THE ROSARY IN 50 PAGES

THE LAYMAN'S QUICK GUIDE TO MARY'S PSALTER

TAYLOR R. MARSHALL

SAINT JOHN PRESS

MMXX

Sacred Scripture citations are generally from the 1899 edition of the Douay-Rheims (Challoner) Bible or a translation of my own rendering.

Marshall, Taylor
The Rosary in Fifty Pages
The Layman's Quick Guide to the Rosary / Taylor Marshall
1st ed.
Includes bibliographical references and index
ISBN:
1. Rosary. 2. Catholicism. 3. Theology. I. Title.

Published by Saint John Press

Printed in the United States of America
Acid-free paper for permanence and durability
Cover Art and Rosary Instruction Design: Steven M. Nelson
{smnelsondesign.com}

Please visit *The Rosary in Fifty Pages* on the web at:

www.taylormarshall.com

This book is dedicated to everyone
who has ever prayed a Rosary for me.

Thank you. -TRM

Ascendit Simon Petrus et traxit rete in terram, plenum magnis piscibus *centum quinquaginta tribus.* Et cum tanti essent, non est scissum rete.

- Evangelium secundum Ioannem xxi, 11

TABLE OF CONTENTS

DOES DEVOTION TO MARY STEAL FROM JESUS?

Christianity is the worship of Our Lord Jesus Christ as the Messiah and Son of the Father. The earliest Christian martyrs received the penalty of death for merely stating *Christos Kyrios*— Christ is Lord. Christianity is Christ-centered, and there is no room for other gods, saviors, or idols. This Christocentric vision has led some to conclude wrongly that honor shown to Mary or others is somehow wrong.

During the Protestant Reformation, a movement to reject any veneration of the Blessed Virgin Mary and of the Saints began. This rejection emerged from the Lutheran principle of "Christ alone." This Protestant worldview perceived Mary and the saints as in competition with Jesus Christ and thereby robbing Christ of His due glory. It's like an apple pie with only eight slices. If Mary receives three slices and the saints receive one slice, then Christ only receives four slices left over. We have robbed Christ of half the pie.

But this is not how the life of love and family operates. If a man marries a woman and they have a baby, his love for his wife does not drop by half when the baby is born. Nor does the woman divide her love by 50 percent with her husband. And when a second child is born, love is not taken from the first child. If this were true, a mother of four children would only love each at 25 percent. This ridiculous zero-sum understanding of love and devotion is not in accordance with the New Testament.

If I love my wife, I love my children. And when I love one child, I show love to my wife. And when my wife cares for all eight children, she still loves and honors me. Her love for one child robs me of nothing. If I love my wife's mother, I love my wife even more so. Therefore, we should not say, "By showing love to the Mother of Christ, you rob Christ!" How wrong. How childish. How selfish. If a king honored your mother, would not his royal act bring honor to your entire family?

The problem is that Martin Luther rejected the teaching of the Apostle Paul that all Christian disciples are "in Christ."[1] When Paul persecuted Christians, Jesus Christ said to him, "Saul, Saul, why persecutest thou me?" (Acts 9:4). Paul was not merely attacking Christians; he was directly attacking Christ. This mystery reveals that Christians dwell within Christ and are constituted in the mystery of His Body. Therefore, if you persecute Saint Stephen, you persecute Jesus Christ. If you show love for Saint Stephen, you show love for Jesus Christ. This is the doctrine of participation in Christ, which I cover at length in my book *The Catholic Perspective on Paul.*[2]

DID THE EARLY CHRISTIANS ASK MARY TO PRAY FOR THEM?

A papyrus from the A.D. 200s preserves the earliest known prayer asking for the intervention of the Blessed Virgin Mary. Written in Greek,

Original Greek Text	English Translation
Ὑπὸ τὴν σὴν εὐσπλαγχνίαν,	Under your compassion,
καταφεύγομεν, Θεοτόκε.	We take refuge, O Theotokos.
Τὰς ἡμῶν ἱκεσίας,	Despise not our petitions in our
μὴ παρίδῃς ἐν περιστάσει,	necessities:
ἀλλ᾽ ἐκ κινδύνων λύτρωσαι ἡμᾶς,	but deliver us from dangers,
μόνη Ἁγνή, μόνη εὐλογημένη.	O only Pure, only Blessed one.

Scholars agree that this prayer is addressed to the Blessed Virgin Mary because her Greek title Θεοτόκε, or "God-birther," is invoked. Moreover, this prayer invokes the exact Greek feminine word for "blessed" used in Luke 1:42 by Saint Elizabeth when she told Mary, "Blessed art thou among women": Εὐλογημένη σὺ ἐν γυναιξίν.

This prayer found on an ancient Egyptian papyrus is a prayer still said daily throughout the world in Coptic, Syriac, Armenian, and Latin. The prayer was known and preserved by spoken tradition for 1,800 years before archeologists found this long-lost papyrus. This means that early Christians asked the Blessed Virgin Mary to pray for them.

TWO KINDS OF PRAYER: DIRECT AND INSTRUMENTAL

In early Christianity there were two kinds of prayer. Prayer can be either direct or instrumental. Through Jesus Christ, I can pray directly to God the Father, as Christ taught us. This is direct prayer. For Catholics, the entire liturgy of the Holy Sacrifice of the Mass is direct prayer. The priest, joined by the people, speaks directly to "God the Father through Jesus Christ our Lord in the unity of the Holy Ghost. Amen."

Instrumental prayer, however, is whenever we ask other people to pray for us to God. They become instruments of prayer. If I say to you, "Please pray for my sick grandmother," I am beseeching you to beseech God on behalf of my grandmother. We can add even more people into this prayer chain, allowing hundreds of people to pray and intercede for one another. We are instruments of prayer, creating a symphony of intercession directly to God.

We read in the Book of the Apocalypse that there are twenty-four elders in Heaven (signifying the Twelve Patriarchs of the Old Testament and the Twelve Apostles of the New Testament) who offer to God the prayers of those still on earth:

> And when he had opened the book, the four living creatures, and the four and twenty ancients fell down before the Lamb, having every one of them harps, and golden vials full of odours, which are the prayers of saints. (Revelation 5:8)

9

Early Christians knew they were still connected to other Christians who had been martyred or died. They believed the deceased saints were alive with Christ in Heaven but remained around us on earth as "a great a cloud of witnesses" (Hebrews 12:1). The network of intercessory prayer expanded into Heaven. They said and wrote things like, "Holy Peter and Paul, pray for us." If we ask our neighbor on earth to pray for us, we can also ask Mary, Peter, Stephen, or even an angel to be an instrument of prayer for us. Everyone in Heaven and earth is directing their direct prayer to Holy Trinity.

Prayer to Mary and the devotion of the Rosary is merely asking her to "Pray for us sinners now and at the hour of our death. Amen." She is the Mother of Jesus. She carried Him in her womb. She birthed Him. She nursed Him. She taught Him. She was instrumental in His first miracle at Cana when she said, "Do whatever He tells you to do" (John 2:5). She stood at the foot of the cross. She loves Him, and she loves us. Christ said from the cross, "Behold thy Mother" (John 19:27), and we believe those special words on the cross apply to all those redeemed by the cross.

DID EARLY CHRISTIANS HONOR MARY?

Devotion to the Blessed Virgin begins with Christ. One of the Ten Commandments reads, "Honor thy father and thy mother." We know that our Christ perfectly honored God the Father. But did He also perfectly honor His earthly human mother? Undoubtedly Christ honored Mary at all moments perfectly with His divinity and humanity.

This is why Catholics believe that Mary is sinless. What is the greatest honor a person could receive? To be saved and filled with the Holy Ghost at the very first moment of embryonic conception, the very first moment of existence. This is what Christ did to honor His mother and fulfill the Ten Commandments. Early Christians testify to this profound love for the Virgin Mary. Saint Irenaeus of Lyons (d. A.D. 202) discussed how the sin of Eve parallels the sanctity of the Virgin Mary. The following quote was written about A.D. 180:

> For as Eve was seduced by the word of [a fallen] angel to flee from God, having rebelled against His Word, so Mary by the word of an angel received the glad tidings that she would bear God by obeying his Word. The former was seduced to disobey God, but the latter was persuaded to obey God, so that the Virgin Mary might become the advocate of the Virgin Eve. As the human race was subjected to death through a virgin, so it was saved by a virgin." (Irenaeus, *Against Heresies* 5, 19)

When Saint Irenaeus wrote, "saved by a virgin," he did not mean that Mary is the savior of mankind. In the Bible, Mary says God is her "savior" (Luke 1:47). The Savior Jesus came to us through her immaculate womb. Hence, Mary saves us instrumentally, not absolutely.

Saint Athanasius (d. A.D. 373), the great defender of the divinity of Christ and the Holy Trinity, also testified to Mary being the greatest of God's creatures and the Ark of the New Covenant:

> O noble Virgin, truly you are greater than any other greatness. For who is your equal in greatness, O dwelling place of God the Word? To whom among all creatures shall I compare you, O Virgin? You are greater than them all O Covenant, clothed with purity instead of gold! You are the Ark in which is found the golden vessel containing the true manna, that is, the flesh in which divinity resides. (Athanasius, *Homily of the Papyrus of Turin,* 71:216)

11

WHERE DID THE HAIL MARY COME FROM?

We see that the earliest and most orthodox theologians of the early Church praised and prayed to the Blessed Virgin Mary. The Rosary is based chiefly on praying the Lord's Prayer (the Our Father) and the Angelic Salutation (the Hail Mary). Both are based on biblical texts. The Our Father was given to us by Jesus Christ, and the Hail Mary is based on two verses in Luke:

> And the angel being come in, said unto her: *Hail, full of grace, the Lord is with thee.* (Luke 1:28)

> And it came to pass, that when Elizabeth heard the salutation of Mary, the infant leaped in her womb. And Elizabeth was filled with the Holy Ghost: And she cried out with a loud voice, and said: *Blessed art thou among women, and blessed is the fruit of thy womb.* (Luke 1:42-43)

From these two passages we derive the Hail Mary prayer by also adding the names "Mary" and "Jesus":

> Hail [Mary], full of grace, the Lord is with thee. Blessed art thou among women, and blessed is the fruit of thy womb[Jesus].

Mary Gave the Rosary to Saint Dominic

In the year 1214, Saint Dominic (A.D. 1170–1221), the founder of the Order of Preachers, was in anguish because he was failing in his attempt to convert the Albigensian Cathar heretics. These dualistic heretics taught that the spirit is good and that all physical matter is evil. They believed in a good God who is spiritual and also a bad demigod who created the physical evil universe. The Cathars identified this sinister demiurge with the Old Testament God and called him *Rex Mundi*, or "King of the World." For them, religion was a battle between the Good Father of Jesus Christ and the evil Jewish demigod, *Rex Mundi*.

These Cathar heretics taught that Christ was never an actual human with a physical body and rejected that He was born of the Virgin Mary. They also rejected the bodily resurrection of Christ and the seven sacraments since they were also tangible. They rejected marriage and believed sex was evil since it entrapped more people in physical bodies. The Albigensian heretics were popular in France, and Saint Dominic had prayerfully committed himself and others to preaching to and converting these heretics to save them from their errors.

Saint Dominic failed miserably in his missionary work among these French heretics. He attributed his failure to his own sinfulness and to the poor example of Catholic clergy and laymen. The heretical preachers lived in extreme poverty, while the Catholic bishops and abbots lived in luxury, rode stately horses, and dressed lavishly. Dominic went alone into the forest for three days, praying for the conversion of these heretics back to the true faith. He flogged his body and scourged his flesh. From the fasting, pain, and exhaustion, he fell into a deep sleep.

Dominic experienced an apparition of Blessed Mother Mary, which thereafter linked Saint Dominic and the Rosary. The

Blessed Virgin Mary appeared with three angels and asked Dominic, "Dear Dominic, do you know which weapon the Blessed Trinity wants to use to reform the world?" Dominic answered that she would know better than him. Mary responded, "I want you to know that, in this kind of warfare, the battering ram has always been the Angelic Psalter, which is the foundation stone of the New Testament. Therefore, if you want to reach these hardened souls and win them over to God, preach my Psalter."[3]

When the Blessed Virgin Mary spoke of the "Psalter," she referred to the 150 Psalms of the Old Testament. Monks of the early church would pray all 150 Psalms daily. Those who could not do so would spread out the Psalter over one week. Others would recite 150 Our Fathers or 150 Hail Marys to complete an easier Quasi-Psalter. Dominic understood that she wanted him to preach 150 Angelic Salutations or Hail Marys.

After seeing this apparition, Saint Dominic preached the Angelic Psalter, or Holy Rosary, to the unconverted Albigensian heretics. The 150 Psalms were divided into fifteen decades, or groups of ten. To each of the fifteen decades was assigned a mystery corresponding to the physical and incarnational reality of Our Lord Jesus Christ. The heretics rejected the incarnation of Christ as physical, and so the sign of Mary—that she bore His physical Body in her womb—became the means of conversion. The fifteen mysteries of the Rosary are grouped into three sets of five decades each.

Joyful Mysteries

1. The Annunciation of the Archangel Gabriel to Mary and the Incarnation of Christ
2. The Visitation of Mary to Elizabeth
3. The Nativity of Christ in Bethlehem
4. The Presentation of Jesus at the Temple

5. The Finding of Jesus in the Temple

Sorrowful Mysteries

6. His Agony in the Garden
7. His Scourging at the Pillar
8. His Crowning with Thorns
9. His Carrying of the Cross
10. The Crucifixion and Death of our Lord

Glorious Mysteries

11. His Resurrection from the Tomb
12. His Ascension into Heaven
13. The Descent of the Holy Ghost on Pentecost
14. The Assumption of Mary's Body and Soul to Heaven
15. The Coronation of the Virgin by the Father, Son, and Holy Ghost

This schedule of guided prayer helped the Albigensian heretics better understand and imitate the virtuous life of our Lord Jesus Christ and the Immaculate and Blessed Mary.

DID MARY GIVE THE ROSARY TO SAINT DOMINIC?
Many contemporary scholars question the traditional origin of the Rosary, or Angelic Psalter. They claim, instead, that the Rosary emerged through the organic development of medieval piety and that Mary did not directly give the Holy Rosary to Saint Dominic. These Modernists hold that the traditional account of Mary giving the Rosary directly to Saint Dominic is an etiological myth that allegorized the origin of the Rosary within the Dominican order.

The "true" story, the Modernists claim, is that the Rosary developed gradually. They say that since the Dominicans popularized the Rosary devotion, the traditional myth personifies the Dominicans in the person of Saint Dominic. So then, the Modernists allege, the Blessed Virgin Mary did not directly give the Rosary to Dominic. Rather, the Dominicans popularized the devotion, and so Mary figuratively gave the Rosary to the world through the "sons of Dominic" (the Dominicans).

Critics rightly observe that the practice of praying Our Fathers and Hail Marys on beads is a practice that predates Saint Dominic. In *The Life of Saint Paul the First Hermit*, written by Saint Jerome (d. A.D. 420), we learn that Saint Paul of Thebes (d. A.D. c. 342) counted his prayers on a knotted cord. A set of prayer beads was found in the tomb of Saint Gertrude of Nivelles (d. A.D. 659) in modern-day Belgium. Prayer beads were also found in the tombs of Saint Norbert (1075-1134) and Saint Rosalia (1130–1166). These examples reveal a preexisting Christian tradition of counting prayers on knotted ropes or beads.

While it is certain that many prayed on beads prior to Saint Dominic, the original claim is that the Immaculate Mother herself gave to Saint Dominic the Holy Rosary as a collection of 150 Hail Marys with the fifteen Mysteries. Even the words of Mary indicate that this tradition existed before Saint Dominic. The legend records Mary saying to Saint Dominic that this practice "has always been":

> I want you to know that, in this kind of warfare, the battering ram *has always been* the Angelic Psalter, which is the foundation stone of the New Testament [emphasis added].[4]

The key to this debate is realizing that the Holy Rosary is not merely praying on beads but praying the 150 Hail Marys with the fifteen corresponding mysteries. It is this special combination of 150 Hail Marys with the fifteen mysteries that constitutes the Rosary, and it is this combination of vocal and mental prayer that Mary gave to Saint Dominic.

WHAT DOES THE CATHOLIC CHURCH SAY?

Pope Leo XIII, in his encyclical *Octobri mense,* teaches that the Rosary was "instituted and propagated" by Saint Dominic "by her command and counsel":

> That the Queen of Heaven herself has granted a great efficacy to this devotion is demonstrated by the fact that it was, by her command and counsel, instituted and propagated by the illustrious Saint Dominic, in times particularly dangerous for the Catholic cause.[5]

Pope Leo XIII also clarified that this institution of the Holy Rosary by Mary included the Joyful, Sorrowful, and Glorious Mysteries, which he calls the "great mysteries of Jesus and Mary, their joys, sorrows, and triumphs."

In his *Supremi Apostolatus Officio,* Pope Leo XIII again confirms the supernatural origin of the Holy Rosary of Saint Dominic:

> Great in the integrity of his doctrine, in his example of virtue, and by his apostolic labors, he proceeded undauntedly to attack the enemies of the Catholic Church, not by force of arms, but trusting wholly to that devotion which he was the first to institute under the name of the Holy Rosary, which was disseminated through the length and breadth of the earth by him and his pupils. Guided, in fact, by divine inspiration and grace, he foresaw that this devotion, like a most powerful warlike weapon, would be the means of putting the enemy to flight, and of confounding their audacity and mad impiety. Such was indeed its result. Thanks to this new method of prayer—when adopted and properly carried out as instituted by the Holy Father Saint Dominic—piety, faith, and union began

to return, and the projects and devices of the heretics to fall to pieces.[6]

The apparition of the Immaculate Mary to Blessed Alanus de Rupe also confirms the tradition:

> My son, you know perfectly the ancient devotion of my Rosary, preached and diffused by your Patriarch and my Servant Dominic and by his spiritual sons, your religious brothers. This spiritual exercise is extremely agreeable to both my Son and to me, and most useful and holy for the faithful. When my Servant Dominic started to preach my Rosary... the reform in the world reached such heights that it seemed that men were transformed into angelic spirits and that Angels had descended from Heaven to inhabit the earth.... No one was considered a true Christian unless he had my Rosary and prayed it.[7]

DOES THE ROSARY PREDATE SAINT DOMINIC?

As stated above, Saint Jerome records that Saint Paul of Thebes prayed on a knotted rope, but he does not tell us what Paul was praying. There is a matching Eastern Orthodox tradition that the fourth century monks of the Egyptian Thebaid were praying 150 Angelic Salutations (Hail Marys) grouped into fifteen decades, following the pattern of the 150 Psalms. Corresponding with this Egyptian tradition is the Eastern Orthodox Rule of the Theotokos, which consists of 150 Hail Marys with fifteen corresponding mysteries.

The evidence for the first two revelations of the Angelic Psalter in fourth century and then the eighth century derive from an Eastern Orthodox priest, Father Zosima, who is the spiritual son of Saint Seraphim of Sarov (1754 or 1759–1833), who said:

I forgot to give you a piece of advice vital for salvation. Say the O Hail, Mother of God and Virgin one hundred and fifty times, and this prayer will lead you on the way to salvation. This rule was given by the Mother of God herself in about the eighth century, and at one time all Christians fulfilled it.

We Orthodox have forgotten about it, and Saint Seraphim has reminded me of this Rule. In my hands I have a handwritten book from the cell of Saint Seraphim, containing a description of the many miracles which took place through praying to the Mother of God and especially through saying one hundred and fifty times the "O Hail, Mother of God and Virgin."

If, being unaccustomed to it, it is difficult to master one hundred and fifty repetitions daily, say it fifty times at first. After every ten repetitions say the "Our Father" once and "Open unto us the doors of thy loving kindness." [8] Whomever he spoke to about this miracle-working Rule remained grateful to him.

Saint Seraphim of Sarov gave one of his spiritual children the task of copying a plan that included his prayer to the Ever-Virgin Mary. Here are the mysteries as preserved in Russia at the beginning of the nineteenth century:

1. First decade. Let us remember the Birth of the Mother of God. Let us pray for mothers, fathers, and children.
2. Second decade. Let us remember the feast of the Presentation of the Blessed Virgin and Mother of God. Let us pray for those who have lost their way and fallen away from the church.

3. Third decade. Let us remember the Annunciation of the Blessed Mother of God. Let us pray for the soothing of sorrows and the consolation of those who grieve.
4. Fourth decade. Let us remember the Visitation of the Blessed Virgin with the righteous Elizabeth. Let us pray for the reunion of the separated, for those whose dear ones or children are living away from them or missing.
5. Fifth decade. Let us remember the Birth of Christ. Let us pray for the rebirth of souls, for new life in Christ.
6. Sixth decade. Let us remember the Feast of the Presentation of the Lord and the words uttered by Saint Simeon: "Yea, a sword shall pierce through thy own soul also" (Luke 2:35). Let us pray that the Mother of God will meet our souls at the hour of our deaths, contrive that we receive the Holy Sacrament with our last breath, and lead our souls through the terrible torments.
7. Seventh decade. Let us remember the flight of the Mother of God with the God-child into Egypt. Let us pray that the Mother of God will help us avoid temptation in this life and deliver us from misfortunes.
8. Eighth decade. Let us remember the disappearance of the twelve-year-old boy Jesus in Jerusalem and the sorrow of the Mother of God on this account. Let us pray, begging the Mother of God for the constant repetition of the Jesus Prayer.
9. Ninth decade. Let us remember the miracle performed in Cana of Galilee, when the Lord turned water into wine at the words of the Mother of God: "They have no wine" (John 2:3). Let us ask the Mother of God for help in our affairs and deliverance from need.
10. Tenth decade. Let us remember the Mother of God standing at the cross of the Lord, when grief pierced through her heart like a sword. Let us pray to the Mother of God for the strengthening of our souls and the banishment of despondency.

11. Eleventh decade. Let us remember the Resurrection of Christ and ask the Mother of God in prayer to resurrect our souls and give us a new courage for spiritual feats.
12. Twelfth decade. Let us remember the Ascension of Christ, at which the Mother of God was present. Let us pray and ask the Queen of Heaven to raise up our souls from earthly and worldly amusements and direct them to striving for higher things.
13. Thirteenth decade. Let us remember the upper room and the descent of the Holy Spirit on the Apostles and the Mother of God. Let us pray: "Create in me a clean heart, O God, and renew a right spirit within me. Cast me not away from thy presence, and take not thy Holy Spirit from me" (Psalm 51).
14. Fourteenth decade. Let us remember the Assumption of the Blessed Mother of God and ask for a peaceful and serene end.
15. Fifteenth decade. Let us remember the glory of the Mother of God, with which the Lord crowned her after her removal from earth to Heaven. Let us pray to the Queen of Heaven not to abandon the faithful who are on earth but to defend them from every evil, covering them with her honoring and protecting veil.

Here is how this Russian Rosary compares to the traditional Rosary of Saint Dominic:

Angelic Psalter of Saint Dominic (Thirteenth Century)	**Rule of the Theotokos of Saint Seraphim** (Nineteenth Century)
1. Annunciation to Mary	1. Nativity of Mary
2. Visitation of Mary to Elizabeth	2. Presentation of Mary in Temple
3. Nativity of Christ	3. Annunciation to Mary
4. Presentation of Christ in	4. Visitation of Mary to

Temple	Elizabeth
5. Finding of Jesus in Temple	5. Nativity of Christ
6. Agony of Christ in the Garden	6. Presentation of Christ in Temple
7. Scourging of Christ	7. Flight of Holy Family to Egypt
8. Crowning with Thorns	8. Finding of Jesus in Temple
9. Carrying the Cross	9. Turning Water into Wine
10. Crucifixion and Death	10. Crucifixion and Death
11. Resurrection of Christ	11. Resurrection of Christ
12. Ascension of Christ	12. Ascension of Christ
13. Descent of the Holy Ghost	13. Descent of the Holy Ghost
14. Assumption of Mary	14. Assumption of Mary
15. Crowning of Mary	15. Crowning of Mary

The first nine mysteries differ, yet the last five mysteries correspond exactly to the Glorious Mysteries in the Dominican tradition. The mysteries for each version are biblical and maintain the structure of 150 Hail Marys, which are in keeping the 150 Psalms. It seems that Our Lady, over and over, leads her children to rediscover the riches of the Rosary. When we pray the Hail Mary and reflect on the mysteries of the life of Christ, we ask Our Lady to help us grow closer to Christ.

THE POWER OF THE ROSARY

Shortly after the death of Saint Dominic in 1221, we find the great Dominican theologian Saint Thomas Aquinas (d. 1274) giving a series of sermons on the topic of the *Ave Maria*, or Hail Mary. The popularity of the Rosary became universal in the 1400s thanks to another Dominican theologian named Alanus de Rupe (1428–1475). Alanus was perhaps the preeminent scholar and preacher of his century. Born in Brittany in around 1428, he joined the Dominican Order at age thirty-one. From 1459 to 1475 he taught theology at prestigious universities in Paris, Lille, Douay, Ghent, and Rostock.

FIFTEEN PROMISES OF THE ROSARY

Circa 1460, Alanus received many visions about the Rosary. He claimed that Mary made fifteen promises to those who prayed the Rosary:

1. Whoever shall faithfully serve me by the recitation of the Rosary shall receive signal graces.
2. I promise my special protection and the greatest graces to all those who shall recite the Rosary.
3. The Rosary shall be a powerful armor against hell, it will destroy vice, decrease sin, and defeat heresies.
4. It will cause virtue and good works to flourish; it will obtain for souls the abundant mercy of God; it will withdraw the heart of men from the love of the world and its vanities, and will lift them to the desire of eternal things. Oh, that souls would sanctify themselves by these means.
5. The soul, which recommends itself to me by the recitation of the Rosary, shall not perish.

6. Whoever shall recite the Rosary devoutly, applying himself to the consideration of its sacred mysteries, shall never be conquered and never overwhelmed by misfortune. God will not chastise him in His justice, and he shall not perish by an unprovided death (unprepared for Heaven). The sinner shall convert. The just shall grow in grace and become worthy of eternal life.
7. Whoever shall have a true devotion for the Rosary shall not die without the sacraments of the Church.
8. Those who are faithful to recite the Rosary shall have, during their life and at their death, the light of God and the plenitude of His graces; at the moment of death they shall participate in the merits of the saints in paradise.
9. I shall deliver from purgatory those who have been devoted to the Rosary.
10. The faithful children of the Rosary shall merit a high degree of glory in Heaven.
11. You shall obtain all you ask of me by the recitation of the Rosary.
12. All those who propagate the Holy Rosary shall be aided by me in their necessities.
13. I have obtained from my Divine Son that all the advocates of the Rosary shall have for intercessors the entire celestial court during their life and at the hour of death.
14. All who recite the Rosary are my children and brothers and sisters of my only son, Jesus Christ.
15. Devotion of my Rosary is a great sign of predestination.

In 1470, Alanus founded the Confraternity of the Psalter of the Glorious Virgin Mary in order to spread devotion to the Rosary throughout Europe. When he died five years later in 1475, he was the undisputed Apostle of the Rosary.

The Hail Mary prayer itself received its final form at this time. The Hail Mary as we say it today first appeared in print in

A.D. 1495 in the Dominican preacher Girolamo Savonarola's *Esposizione sopra l'Ave Maria*:

> Hail Mary, full of grace, the Lord is with thee; blessed art thou amongst women, and blessed is the fruit of thy womb, Jesus. Holy Mary, Mother of God, pray for us sinners, now and at the hour of our death. Amen.

No one can doubt the origin and propagation of the Holy Rosary from within the Dominican Order of Preachers. The development became officially established in A.D. 1569 when the Dominican Pope Saint Pius V (1504-1572) issued the papal bull *Consueverunt Romani Pontifices*, thereby confirming the official configuration of 150 Hail Marys and fifteen mysteries of the Holy Rosary:

> And so Dominic looked to that simple way of praying and beseeching God, accessible to all and wholly pious, which is called the Rosary, or Psalter of the Blessed Virgin Mary, in which the same most Blessed Virgin is venerated by the angelic greeting repeated one hundred and fifty times, that is, according to the number of the Davidic Psalter, and by the Lord's Prayer with each decade. Interposed with these prayers are certain meditations showing forth the entire life of Our Lord Jesus Christ, thus completing the method of prayer devised by the Fathers of the Holy Roman Church.

ROSARY AT THE BATTLE OF LEPANTO

Two years later in 1571, Pope Pius V begged all of Christendom to pray the Rosary while a coalition of European Catholic maritime states sailed from Sicily against the powerful Turkish fleet in the Battle of Lepanto. The Christian fleet was greatly outnumbered. If the Turks won, they would initiate a naval invasion of Italy and take Rome. The Turkish sultan had already dubbed himself as the emperor of Romans. This battle, if lost, would lead to Muslim rule over Rome, and from Rome, the Sultan could conquer the rest of Europe.

After five hours of sea battle off the western coast of Greece, the combined navies of the Papal States, Venice, and Spain defeated the Ottoman Turks. Pope Pius V received a vision in which he saw the Christian forces take the victory. He commanded the bells of Rome to be rung in victory.

The navies of this Holy League credited the victory to the Virgin Mary and the prayers of the Holy Rosary. It's also worth noting that the Genoese admiral, Andrea Doria, kept in his stateroom a copy of the miraculous image of the then-recent apparition of Our Lady of Guadalupe, given to him by King Philip II of Spain. Pope Pius V instituted a new Catholic feast day of Our Lady of Victory to commemorate the battle on October 7.

In 1573, Pope Gregory XIII changed the title of the Feast of Our Lady of Victory to Feast of the Holy Rosary. Dominican friar Juan Lopez, in his 1584 book on the Rosary, states that the feast of the Rosary was celebrated "in memory and in perpetual gratitude of the miraculous victory that the Lord gave to his Christian people that day against the Turkish armada."[9]

SECRET OF THE ROSARY

The Protestant Reformation initiated by Martin Luther in 1517 was not originally anti-Marian. Martin Luther taught that the Blessed Virgin Mary was the Theotokos, the Ever-Virgin, and was without sin through her Immaculate Conception.[10] He originally held that Mary was able to pray for us as a mother before Christ, but he later rejected this Catholic understanding and rejected all instrumental requests for the prayers of the saints and of Mary. Subsequent Reformers, such as Ulrich Zwingli, John Calvin, Martin Bucer, Thomas Cranmer, and the Anabaptists, violently rejected devotion to the Blessed Virgin Mary and the saints.

Devotion to the Holy Rosary entirely disappeared wherever Protestantism took root.

Catholics during the Reformation were challenged with the Protestant claim that we are must focus on "Christ alone." There was a fear that ignorant laymen might love and serve Mary or a certain saint more than they would the Lord Jesus Christ. Although the Catholic Church defended the veneration (not adoration or worship) of Mary and the saints and instrumental requests for their prayers, there was a counter-movement within the Catholic Church to downplay Mary and the saints: Jansenism.

Cornelius Jansen (1585–1638) was a well-revered theologian and Catholic bishop in Flanders. His followers, called Jansenists, formed a powerful theological movement in the Low Countries and in France that revered the writings of Saint Augustine and thereby emphasized the doctrines of original sin and predestination. Their Catholic opponents saw the Jansenists as the Catholic version of Calvinism, and although the Jansenists did not reject veneration of Mary and the saints, they did discourage these forms of piety.

The Jansenists, like the Calvinists, emphasized the divinity of Christ and deemphasized His humanity. The struggle against Jansenism from in the seventeenth and eighteenth centuries centered on fostering popular devotion to the infancy of Christ, the humanity of Christ, the crucifixion of Christ, and the Blessed Virgin Mary's role as the Mother of the Son of God and provider of His sacred humanity.

Saint Louis-Marie Grignion de Montfort (1673–1716) was a pivotal figure in this devotional movement against Jansenism. He was a popular French priest and preacher who was made a missionary apostolic by Pope Clement XI. His battles with the Jansenists were well known. He and his devotees constructed an enormous crucifix, only for it to be destroyed on the orders of the King of France under the influence of the Jansenists.

Saint Louis de Montfort's primary weapon against Jansenism was the Holy Rosary. In 1700, he joined the Third Order of Saint Dominic and became an ardent apostle of the Rosary. His two notable books are *True Devotion to Mary* and *Secret of the Rosary*. In the first book, he defends the theological principle that the Son of God came to save humanity through Mary and that this incarnational principle establishes an everlasting principle of going "to Jesus through Mary." Saint Louis de Montfort explains that one can never have too much devotion to Mary because Christ as the Son of God already has exhausted the amount of devotion that one could show for Mary, as He fulfills the commandment "Honor thy mother." We merely attempt to imitate Him. There is, then, a distinction between the kind of adoration that God alone receives, and the kind of veneration that creatures like Mary and the Saints may receive.

The Catholic Ecumenical Council of Nicea II (A.D. 787) dogmatically distinguished between three kinds of worship. We worship the Father, the Son, and the Holy Ghost only with adoration (Greek: *latria*) and instead show human veneration (Greek: *dulia*) for the saints. Mary, as the greatest saint and Mother of the Son of God, receives "highest veneration" (Greek: *hyperdulia*).

If God gave us Jesus Christ through Mary, then "to Jesus through Mary" becomes a pattern established by God. This opens the way to total consecration to Jesus through Mary, since a total consecration to Mary is actually only a means or a bridge of total consecration to Jesus through Mary. Nothing ends in Mary, it always moves on "to Jesus."

Saint Louis de Montfort also authored *Secret of the Rosary*, which is a history of the Rosary from Saint Dominic up through Blessed Alanus de Rupe and many other admirable stories about the power of the Rosary. It explains the mysteries and how to pray the Rosary effectively. He emphasizes the importance of the fifteen mysteries and the use of mental prayer and reflective pauses during the Rosary. De Montfort's *Secret of the Rosary* is the classic devotional treatise on the Rosary. It should be the next book you read after this one.

LEO XIII: POPE OF THE ROSARY

The works of Saint Louis de Montfort were lost for 126 years after his death in 1716 and were not found again until 1842. When they were recovered, the Catholic Church was still under internal and external attacks stemming, in part, from the French Revolution. Beset at every side, Catholics turned to a deeper devotion to Jesus Christ through Mary. Four events contributed to this renewed devotion to Mary:

- **1842.** The writings of Saint Louis de Montfort were discovered.
- **1846.** The apparition of Our Lady of La Salette.
- **1854.** Pope Pius IX promulgated *Ineffabilis Deus*, dogmatizing the Immaculate Conception
- **1858.** The apparition of Our Lady of Lourdes.

In 1878, Cardinal Pecci was elected bishop of Rome and chose the name Pope Leo XIII. He went on to become the Pope of the Rosary by issuing twelve encyclicals and five apostolic letters about the Holy Rosary. The rediscovered books of Saint Louis de Montfort had a profound impact on the Marian spirituality of Pope Leo XIII. This is evident by the fact that this pope attached an indulgence to anyone who consecrated himself to Mary using the consecration method of Saint Louis de Montfort. He also inserted the invocation "Queen of the Most Holy Rosary" to the Litany of Loreto. He composed the Saint Michael Prayer, which is almost universally prayed at the end of the Rosary.[11]

Pope Leo XIII dedicated the month of October to the Rosary since October 7 is the feast of Our Lady of the Rosary. He also expanded the indulgences attached to praying the Rosary. He oversaw the erection of the Basilica of the Rosary in Lourdes and supported the Rosary apostolate of Blessed Bartolo Longo at the Basilica of the Rosary in Pompeii.

A SATANIST BECOMES APOSTLE OF THE ROSARY

From the 1840s to the 1860s, the Catholic Church was under attack by secular nationalist forces aligned with Freemasonry, the occult, and secret societies. During this time, Italian General Giuseppe Garibaldi desired a united Italy without the pope. He and other secularists wanted a secular regime divorced from the papacy and Catholicism and united through secular humanism and the occult. Throughout Europe, but especially in Italy, people began to dabble with witchcraft, occultism, and séances.

One such person was Bartolo Longo. As a law student at the University of Naples, he was drawn to the political revolutionary spirit on campus. His advocacy for a united and secular Italy naturally fit with this rise in occult mysticism and his affiliation with a Satanic cult. As a practitioner of Satanism, he was eventually ordained as a Satanic priest.

The young Bartolo began to suffer from "depression, nervousness, and confusion" and became suicidal.[12] A Catholic friend of Longo convinced him that his paranoia was due his involvement with the occult and Satanism. This friend, Vincenzo Pepe, arranged for Longo to meet the Dominican Father Alberto Radente. At the age of thirty, on the feast of Our Lady of the Rosary in 1871, Bartolo Longo, dedicated himself to God as a Dominican tertiary and took the name Rosario. To renounce the occult, Bartolo interrupted a séance by holding up a Rosary and proclaiming, "I renounce spiritualism because it is nothing but a maze of error and falsehood." He then established the Confraternity of the Rosary to promote devotion to God through the Rosary.

Bartolo received a painting of Our Lady of the Rosary giving the Rosary to Saint Dominic and Saint Catherine of Siena. The image was placed in a restored church and became a destination for pilgrims after miracles were reported. The bishop of Nola approved the construction of a larger church. Work on the church began May 8, 1876, and the church was consecrated in May 1891 by Cardinal La Valletta, who represented Pope Leo XIII. Today it is known as the Basilica of Our Lady of the Most Holy Rosary of Pompei. The Italian mystic and stigmatist Saint Padre Pio (1887-1968) was very devoted to this image and the basilica housing it.

It was a miracle of divine grace that a Satanic priest became an Apostle of the Rosary in just five years, from 1871 to 1876. This confirms that the Rosary, as a prayerful mediation on the biblical mysteries of the Gospels, is the best and quickest route to Jesus Christ. At the suggestion of the Pope of the Rosary, Pope Leo XIII, Bartolo Longo and the Countess Mariana di Fusco married on April 7, 1885. They observed a Josephite marriage, whereby they abstained entirely from intercourse and spent their time and resources on caring for the poor and for orphans.

OUR LADY OF FATIMA AND THE ROSARY

On May 13, 1917, the Blessed Virgin Mary appeared to three children, Lúcia, Francisco, and Jacinta, while they were tending sheep at the Cova da Iria near in the parish of Fatima, Portugal. The children agreed to pray the Rosary together after eating their packed lunches around noon. The children had an abbreviated version of the Rosary that only the first words of each prayer: "Our Father," "Hail Mary," and so on.

As a thunderstorm rolled across the horizon, a flash of lightning struck near them, and they saw a lady wearing a white mantle with gilded edges. In her hand was a shining Rosary with a crucifix that gleamed like a precious stone. This lady was "shining brighter than the sun, giving out rays of clear and intense light, just like a crystal goblet full of pure water when the fiery sun passes through it."[13]

"PRAY THE ROSARY EVERY DAY"

The lady tenderly instructed the children: "I want you to return here on the thirteenth of each month for the next six months, and at the very same hour. Later I shall tell you who I am, and what it is that I most desire. And I shall return here yet a seventh time."

"And shall I go to Heaven?"

"Yes, you will," answered the Lady.

"And Jacinta?"

"She will go too."

"And Francisco?"

"Francisco, too, my dear, but he will first have many Rosaries to say."

For a moment the Lady looked at Francisco with compassion. Lúcia then remembered some friends who had died: "Is Maria Neves in Heaven?"

"Yes, she is."

"And Amelia?"

"She is in purgatory. Will you offer yourselves to God, and bear all the suffering He sends you, in atonement for all the sins that offend Him and for the conversion of sinners?"

"Oh, we will! We will!"

"Then you will have a great deal to suffer, but the grace of God will be with you and will strengthen you."

The Blessed Mother then told them: "Pray the Rosary every day to bring peace to the world and an end to the war."

"I AM THE LADY OF THE ROSARY"

Over the next five months, the woman would appear as promised on the thirteenth day of the month. Even though it meant they would be persecuted by local civil authorities, people gathered with the children each and every time, and all would pray the Rosary together.

It was raining on October 13, 1917, the final day the Lady was to appear. Both skeptics and faithful pilgrims slogged through the muddy field. Newspapers and those present estimated that the crowd that day numbered 50,000 to 75,000. The children led the crowd in the Rosary at noon, and then the Lady appeared once again.

Lúcia asked, "What do you want of me?"

"I want a chapel built here in my honor. I want you to continue saying the Rosary every day. The war will end soon, and the soldiers will return to their homes."

"Yes. Yes. Will you tell me your name?" Lúcia asked.

"I am the Lady of the Rosary."

Lúcia continued, "I have many petitions from many people. Will you grant them?"

"Some I shall grant, and others I must deny. People must amend their lives and ask pardon for their sins. They must not offend our Lord anymore, for He is already too much offended!"

"And is that all you have to ask?"

"There is nothing more."

Lúcia recalled that the Lady then rose toward the east and turned her palms toward the dark sky. The dark clouds blocking the sun's rays opened up, and light burst forth as the sun spun like a plate.

"Look at the sun!"

THE MIRACLE OF THE SUN

The crowd of at least 50,000 onlookers then watched the sun dance in the sky. National newspapers (even those aligned with Marxism and Freemasonry) published the events surrounding of the Miracle of the Sun. Locally and around the world, people were converted back to Jesus Christ in the Catholic Church. Many eyewitness accounts have been collected and published. They each describe the sun "dancing" in the sky by spinning, zigzagging, and moving up and down in the sky, with the colors of the rainbow displayed. The soggy and muddy ground from the rains that day miraculously became dry again, as did the clothing of the wet witnesses.

Besides this miracle of the sun, Lúcia also saw three apparitions signifying the three sets of mysteries in the Rosary.

First, she saw Saint Joseph with the Holy Child and Our Lady in her blue mantle. Joseph and the Holy Child blessed the crowd by making the sign of the cross. The Holy Family here signifies the Joyful Mysteries that included the infancy of Jesus Christ in the home of Joseph and Mary.

Secondly, Lúcia saw Our Lord in His Passion and Our Lady of Sorrows, which means that this second vision signifies the Sorrowful Mysteries of Christ suffering and Our Lady accompanying Him in His Passion.

Third, Lúcia saw the Blessed Virgin Mary as our Lady of Carmel. The depiction of Our Lady of Mount Carmel signifies the glorious Queenship of Mary. In the Old Testament, the story of Mount Carmel signifies the glorious triumph of God against His enemies (see the story of Elijah against the prophets of Baal in 3 Kings 18).

The Lady waited to reveal her title as this apparition, and she called herself the Lady of the Rosary. From day one, the mystery of Fatima began with the children praying the Rosary, and also with the Blessed Virgin Mary asking that the Rosary be prayed by all daily. She always appeared to the children while holding the Rosary. This devotion, established in 1214 by Saint Dominic, had become the central feature of the most-witnessed miracle since the parting of the Red Sea by Moses. The Blessed Virgin Mary left Heaven in 1917 to visit Portugal and warn the world of the Second World War, and her remedy was fidelity to Jesus, repentance, and the Holy Rosary.

Saints and Popes on the Rosary

† "If you persevere in reciting the Rosary, this will be a most probable sign of your eternal salvation" (Blessed Alanus de Rupe).

† "The greatest method of praying is to pray the Rosary" (Saint Francis de Sales).

† "Never will anyone who says his Rosary every day be led astray. This is a statement that I would gladly sign with my blood" (Saint Louis de Montfort)

† "When the Holy Rosary is said well, it gives Jesus and Mary more glory and is more meritorious than any other prayer" (Saint Louis de Montfort).

† "If you say the Rosary faithfully unto death, I do assure you that, in spite of the gravity of your sins, you will receive a never-fading crown of glory" (Saint Louis de Montfort).

† "The Rosary is a priceless treasure inspired by God" (Saint Louis De Montfort).

† "Recite your Rosary with faith, with humility, with confidence, and with perseverance" (Saint Louis de Montfort).

† "Give me an army saying the Rosary and I will conquer the world" (Pope Pius IX).

† "The Rosary is the most excellent form of prayer and the most efficacious means of attaining eternal life. It is the remedy for all our evils, the root of all our blessings. There is no more excellent way of praying" (Saint Leo XIII).

† "Of all prayers the Rosary is the most beautiful and the richest in graces ... love the Rosary and recite it every day with devotion" (Saint Pius X).

† "The Rosary is a powerful weapon to put the demons to flight and to keep oneself from sin... If you desire peace in your hearts, in your homes, and in your country, assemble each evening to recite the Rosary. Let not even one day pass without saying it, no matter how burdened you may be with many cares and labors" (Pope Pius XI).

† "There is no surer means of calling down God's blessings upon the family... than the daily recitation of the Rosary" (Pope Pius XII).

† "Our Lady has never refused me a grace through the recitation of the Rosary" (Saint Padre Pio).

† "The Rosary is the weapon for these times" (Saint Padre Pio).

† "Some people are so foolish that they think they can go through life without the help of the Blessed Mother. Love the Madonna and pray the Rosary, for her Rosary is the weapon against the evils of the world today. All graces given by God pass through the Blessed Mother" (Saint Padre Pio).

† "Go to the Madonna. Love her! Always say the Rosary. Say it well. Say it as often as you can! Be souls of prayer. Never tire of praying, it is what is essential. Prayer shakes the Heart of God, it obtains necessary graces!" (Saint Padre Pio).

† "The Rosary is the book of the blind, where souls see and there enact the greatest drama of love the world has ever known; it is the book of the simple, which initiates them into mysteries and knowledge more satisfying than the education of other men; it is the book of the aged, whose eyes close upon the shadow of this world, and open on the substance of the next. The power of the Rosary is beyond description" (Archbishop Fulton Sheen).

† "The Most Holy Virgin in these last times in which we live has given a new efficacy to the recitation of the Rosary to such an extent that there is no problem, no matter how difficult it is, whether temporal or above all spiritual, in the personal life of

each one of us, of our families...that cannot be solved by the Rosary. There is no problem, I tell you, no matter how difficult it is, that we cannot resolve by the prayer of the Holy Rosary" (Saint Lúcia dos Santos of Fatima).

† "Here is an example to help you understand the efficacy of the Rosary. You remember the story of David who vanquished Goliath. What steps did the young Israelite take to overthrow the giant? He struck him in the middle of the forehead with a pebble from his sling. If we regard the Philistine as representing evil and all its powers: heresy, impurity, pride, we can consider the little stones from the sling capable of overthrowing the enemy as symbolizing the Aves of the Rosary" (Blessed Columba Marmion).

HOW TO PRAY THE ROSARY

The essence of praying the Rosary is meditating on the mysteries that are assigned to each set of ten beads, which we call a decade of beads. Our Lady originally called this prayer the Angelic Psalter. It is angelic since the angel Gabriel recited the first hail to Mary in Luke 1:28. It is the Psalter because it consists of 150 Hail Marys, just as the Old Testament contains 150 Psalms of David. In order to pace the prayers throughout the 150 prayers, the division of fifteen decades provides intervals of progress and a new mystery for every ten Hail Marys.

THE BIBLE ON BEADS

The Rosary is the Bible on beads. When you pray the Rosary, you are meditating on the fifteen mysteries of Christ's life, death, and resurrection, as well as Christ giving to Mary her "never fading crown of glory" (1 Peter 5:4). Beyond these fifteen mysteries, the Rosary structure is built on these prayers:

† The Apostles Creed
† Our Father
† Hail Mary
† Glory Be
† O My Jesus
† Hail Holy Queen

These prayers are printed out in English and Latin at the back of this book in the Appendix. They fit onto the beads as shown in this diagram:

38

15. *Hail Mary*

16. *Glory Be*
17. *Oh My Jesus*
18. *Fourth Mystery,*
Our Father

14. *Declare Third*
Mystery, Our Father
13. *Oh My Jesus*
12. *Glory Be*

19. *Hail Mary*

11. *Hail Mary*

20. *Glory Be*
21. *Oh My Jesus*
22. *Fifth Mystery,*
Our Father

10. *Second Mystery,*
Our Father
9. *Oh My Jesus*
8. *Glory Be*

23. *Hail Mary*

24. *Glory Be*
25. *Oh My Jesus*
26. *Final Prayers*

END

7. *Hail Mary*

6. *Declare First Mystery, Our Father*

5. *Glory Be*

4. *Hail Mary*

3. *Our Father*

1. *Sign of the Cross*

BEGIN

2. *Apostles Creed*

Tips for Praying the Rosary

In his book *The Secret of the Rosary*, Saint Louis de Montfort describes "roses" of practical advice to focus your heart in prayer on the fifteen mysteries:

1. **Purity of Intention (Forty-First Rose)** Do I pray because I love God? Am I in a state of grace or a state of sin? Am I prepared to receive gifts and graces from God?"
2. **With Attention (Forty-Second Rose).** "How can I expect God to listen to me if I do not pay attention to what we are saying?" Think of yourself as speaking to a king and a queen.
3. **Fighting Distractions (Forty-Third Rose).** We always experience internal and external distractions. Do not worry about this. But you should carry to intention to always return your gaze on Jesus whenever distracted away from Him.
4. **A Good Method (Forty-Fourth Rose).** Dedicate each Rosary to a specific intention. You can have one big intention for the Rosary, or you can place five intentions on each of the Mysteries. Don't waste your prayers. Hang intentions upon them.
5. **With Reverence (Forty-Fifth Rose).** De Montfort recommends praying the Rosary while kneeling or by assuming a respectful position. He also recommends breaking it up into pieces. There is no rule that it should be said all at once. A Christian could pray two decades upon waking and then do one at lunch and two before bed.
6. **Group Recitation (Forty-Sixth Rose).** Saint Louis de Montfort teaches that a group Rosary is more powerful. He explains that when one Christian prays the Rosary alone, he gains the merit of one Rosary. But a Christian who prays the Rosary in a group gains merit for all the

Rosaries prayed by each person. Ten people? Ten Rosaries!

7. **Four Proper Dispositions (Forty-Seventh Rose).** De Montfort outlines four proper dispositions: The first disposition is to always pray and not grow faint. The second is to pray the Rosary with faith; the third, with humility; the fourth, with great confidence for the graces for which we pray.

8. **Perseverance (Forty-Eight Rose).** De Montfort says, "God's munificence is shown in His making us seek and ask for, over a long period of time, the grace which He wishes to give us, and quite often the more precious the grace, the longer He takes to grant it." Also, everyone experiences fatigue and frustration in prayer. The Psalms reveal this. But perseverance unto death is what God desires to see in us.

9. **Indulgences (Forty-Ninth Rose).** The Catholic should intend to receive all indulgences attached to the Rosary. A plenary indulgence may be gained if the Rosary "is prayed in Church, in a family group, or in a religious community" and if the following are completed: "a sacramental confession, a Eucharistic Communion, and prayers for the Pope's intentions. In addition, one must be free of all attachments to sin, even venial sin."[14]

10. **Different Methods (Fiftieth Rose).** De Montfort suggests a variety of ways to pray the Rosary. He encourages praying the *Veni Sancte Spiritus* (Come Holy Ghost). He suggests making a statement of intention before each decade: "We offer Thee, O Lord Jesus, this first decade in honor of Thy Incarnation, and we ask of Thee, through this mystery and through the intercession of Thy most Holy Mother, a profound humility." One can also add prayers and statements like this after the decade or during the decade.

41

Other suggestions from saints and spiritual masters:

† Place yourself before an icon of Jesus and Mary.

† Light a candle and dim the lights.

† Pray in a quiet place, a church, or a chapel.

† Pray with the same Rosary beads every day.

† Write out or speak out your intentions for this Rosary.

† Kiss the crucifix or beads out of devotion.

† Carry a Rosary always so you have one whenever you need to pray.

† One decade prayed devoutly is better than five prayed without any devotion.

VARIOUS VERSIONS OF THE ROSARY

LUMINOUS MYSTERIES

But what about the Luminous Mysteries? On October 16, 2002, Pope John Paul II, in his apostolic letter *Rosarium Virginis Mariae*, recommended five new Mysteries to the Rosary, to be prayed on Thursdays. These Mysteries of Light, or Luminous Mysteries, focus on five key moments in the public ministry of our Lord Jesus Christ:

1. The Baptism in the Jordan
2. The Marriage Feast at Cana
3. The Proclamation of the Kingdom
4. The Transfiguration
5. The Institution of the Eucharist

The addition of five to the original fifteen does create a break with the traditional identity of the Rosary as Mary's Psalter of 150 Hail Marys. Pope John Paul II noted this disjunction:

> The selection was determined by the origin of the prayer, which was based on the number 150, the number of the Psalms in the Psalter. I believe, however, that to bring out fully the Christological depth of the Rosary it would be suitable to make an addition to the traditional pattern which, while left to the freedom of individuals and communities, could broaden it to include the mysteries of Christ's public ministry between his Baptism and his Passion.[15]

Some have incorrectly concluded that John Paul II *mandated* a change to the Rosary, but he specifically suggests it under a heading titled "A proposed addition to the traditional pattern" and writes that the Luminous Mysteries are provided "without prejudice to any essential aspect of the prayer's traditional format."[16] It is a proposal "left to the freedom of individuals and communities." I see nothing wrong at all with the Luminous Mysteries, but the traditional arrangement of "Mary's Psalter" with the Fifteen Mysteries as given by Our Lady should be retained as primary and "traditional," as the pope wrote. The Luminous Mysteries are proposed, not mandated, as a prompt to deeper devotion to the ministry of Christ.

FRANCISCAN CROWN ROSARY

The Franciscan Rosary consists of seven sets of ten beads and dates back to the early fifteenth century. A devout young man named Jacobus made it his custom to adorn a beautiful statue of Mary with a crown of freshly picked flowers. He later entered the Franciscan Order of the Friars Minor and was no longer able to continue his devotion. Distraught, he sought to leave the Franciscans and return to the world.

Our Lady then appeared to him and convinced him not to leave the Order. She told him not be troubled because he was no longer permitted to adorn her statue with flowers. Instead of giving her a crown of fresh flowers, which wither, he would weave a crown of prayers, and these prayers could be offered at any moment. This is why it is also called the Crown Rosary. This is the origin of the Rosary of the Seven Joys, which are:

1. The Annunciation
2. The Visitation
3. The Birth of Our Lord Jesus Christ
4. The Adoration of the Magi
5. The Finding of the Child Jesus in the Temple
6. The Appearance of Christ to Mary after the Resurrection

44

7. The Assumption and Coronation of Mary as Queen of Heaven

The seven sets of ten beads add up to seventy Hail Marys, and Franciscans add two more Hail Marys to bring the number to the sacred seventy-two, the age they believe Mary was when she was assumed into Heaven.

During Lent, the Franciscans instead pray the Seven Sorrows of Our Lady, which is identical to the Servite Rosary of the Seven Sorrows of Mary.

SERVITE ROSARY OF THE SEVEN SORROWS OF MARY

In 1233, seven men belonging to a Florentine confraternity devoted to Mary were gathered in prayer under Alessio Falconieri. According to tradition, Mary appeared to the young men and exhorted them to devote themselves to her service and retire from the world. They retired to the deserted slopes of Monte Senario near Florence, where they experienced a second vision of Mary. There they formed a new order called the Servants of Mary and called themselves Servites in recognition of their special manner of venerating Our Lady of Sorrows. The seven weeks, not decades, of the Servite Rosary recalls the Seven Sorrows of the Blessed Virgin Mary:

1. The Prophecy of Simeon
2. The Flight to Egypt
3. The Loss of the Child Jesus for three days
4. Mary meets Jesus carrying the cross
5. The Crucifixion of Jesus
6. The Body of Christ is taken down from the cross and placed in the arms of Mary
7. The Body of Christ is placed in the tomb

A set of introductory prayers for the Servite Rosary was written by Saint Alphonsus Liguori in his book *The Glories of Mary*.

THE BRIDGETTINE ROSARY

The Bridgettine Rosary was instituted by Saint Bridget of Sweden (1303–1373). This six-decade Rosary is traditional in the Discalced Carmelite Order. The Bridgettine Rosary consists of ten Hail Marys prayed on six mysteries, each for the Joyful, the Sorrowful, and the Glorious mysteries. This means that the Bridgettine Rosary has eighteen mysteries in total—three more than the traditional Dominican Rosary:

1. The Immaculate Conception of Mary (added to the Joyful Mysteries).
2. Christ taken down from the cross and placed in Mary's arms (added to the Sorrowful Mysteries).
3. The Patronage of Mary, Queen and Beauty of Carmel (added to the Glorious Mysteries).

The other fifteen mysteries match those of the standard Dominican Rosary. At the end of each decade, however, the Apostle's Creed, not the Glory Be, is recited. The Bridgettine Rosary was indulgenced by Pope Leo X in 1515, by Clement XI in 1716, and by Benedict XIV in 1743. Sadly, it is rarely prayed today.

OTHER ROSARIES AND CHAPLETS

There are over a dozen of other Rosaries and chaplets that are prayed. They include:
1. Chaplet of Black Madonna of Czestochowa, made of nine beads with a crucifix and a medal of Our Lady of Czestochowa.
2. Chaplet of Our Lady, Star of the Sea, consisting of a medal of Our Lady of Mount Carmel, three separate beads, and twelve additional beads.

3. Chaplet of Saint Anthony, made of thirteen sets of three beads.
4. Chaplet of Saint Joseph, which is divided into fifteen groups of four beads consisting of one white and three purple beads.
5. Chaplet of Saint Michael the Archangel, comprised of nine groups of four beads each, consisting of three Hail Marys and one Our Father in each. (Each of the nine groups is said in honor of one of the nine choirs of angels.)
6. Chaplet of Saint Patrick, made of twelve beads symbolizing the twelve perils of St. Patrick.
7. Chaplet of Saint Philomena, consisting of three white beads and thirteen red beads.
8. Chaplet of the Five Wounds of Jesus.
9. Chaplet of the Holy Child Jesus.
10. Chaplet of the Holy Wounds, revealed by Jesus to the Venerable Marie Martha Chambon.
11. Chaplet of the Immaculate Conception, also called the Crown of Stars, consisting of three groups of four beads, with a medal of the Immaculate Conception.
12. Chaplet of the Precious Blood, consisting of thirty-three beads in seven groups.
13. Chaplet of the Sacred Heart, consisting of thirty-three small beads, six large beads, a centerpiece, a crucifix, and a Sacred Heart medal.
14. Chaplet of the Way of the Cross, made of fifteen groups of three beads.
15. Little Chaplet of the Holy Face, which honors the Five Wounds of Jesus Christ and is composed of a cross, six large beads, and thirty-three small beads.
16. Little Flower Chaplet, made of one large bead and twenty-four smaller beads.

There are many chaplets and several more that don't have church approval. Souls can be overburdened or confused by the proliferation of chaplets. It is best to stick with the traditional Dominican Rosary unless one belongs to a religious order that regularly uses a different form, such as the Crown Rosary of the Franciscans.

If you benefited from this book, please take a moment to pray a Hail Mary for the author and review this book on amazon.com. I appreciate you and thank you.

Pray the Rosary every day, or you're not on the team.

—Dr. Taylor Marshall

PRAYERS OF THE ROSARY IN ENGLISH AND LATIN

Below are the prayers you need to pray the Rosary. The English is provided first and then the corresponding prayer in Latin:

SIGN OF THE CROSS—SIGNUM CRUCIS
In the Name of the Father and of the Son and of the Holy Ghost. Amen.

In nomine Patris, et Filii, et Spiritus Sancti. Amen.

APOSTLES' CREED—SYMBOLUM APOSTOLORUM
I believe in God, the Father Almighty, Creator of Heaven and earth, and in Jesus Christ, His only Son, our Lord. He was conceived by the Holy Ghost and born of the Virgin Mary. He suffered under Pontius Pilate, was crucified, died, and was buried. He descended into Hell. On the third day He rose again. He ascended into Heaven and is seated at the right hand of God, the Father Almighty. He will come again to judge the living and the dead.

I believe in the Holy Ghost, the Holy Catholic Church, the communion of saints, the forgiveness of sins, the resurrection of the body, and life everlasting. Amen.

Credo in Deum Patrem omnipoténtem, Creatórem cæli et terræ. Et in Iesum Christum, Fílium eius únicum, Dóminum nostrum, qui concéptus est de Spíritu Sancto, natus ex María Vírgine, passus sub Póntio Piláto, crucifíxus, mórtuus, et sepúltus, descéndit ad ínfernos, tértia die resurréxit a mórtuis, ascéndit ad cælos, sedet ad déxteram Dei Patris omnipoténtis, inde ventúrus est iudicáre vivos et mórtuos.

Credo in Spíritum Sanctum, sanctam Ecclésiam cathólicam, sanctórum communiónem, remissiónem peccatórum, carnis resurrectiónem, vitam ætérnam. Amen.

OUR FATHER—PATER NOSTER

Our Father, Who art in Heaven, hallowed be Thy Name. Thy Kingdom come, Thy will be done on earth, as it is in Heaven. Give us this day our daily bread, and forgive us our trespasses as we forgive those who trespass against us. And lead us not into temptation, but deliver us from evil. Amen.

Pater noster, qui es in cælis, sanctificétur nomen tuum. Advéniat regnum tuum. Fiat volúntas tua, sicut in cælo, et in terra. Panem nostrum quotidiánum da nobis hódie, et dimítte nobis débita nostra sicut et nos dimíttimus debitóribus nostris. Et ne nos indúcas in tentatiónem, sed líbera nos a malo. Amen.

HAIL MARY—AVE MARIA

Hail Mary, full of Grace, the Lord is with thee.
Blessed art thou amongst women, and blessed is the fruit of Thy womb, Jesus.
Holy Mary, Mother of God, pray for us sinners, now and in the hour of our death. Amen.

Ave María, grátia plena, Dóminus tecum.
Benedícta tu in muliéribus, et benedíctus fructus ventris tui, Iesus.
Sancta María, Mater Dei, ora pro nobis peccatóribus, nunc, et in hora mortis nostræ. Amen.

GLORY BE—GLORIA PATRI

Glory be to the Father, and to the Son, and to the Holy Ghost.
As it was in the beginning, is now, and ever shall be, world without end. Amen.

Glória Patri, et Fílio, et Spirítui Sancto.

Sicut erat in princípio, et nunc, et semper, et in sǽcula sæculórum. Amen.

FATIMA PRAYER: O MY JESUS

O my Jesus, forgive us our sins and save us from the fires of Hell. Lead all souls to Heaven, especially those in most need of Thy mercy.

Dómine Jesu, dimitte nobis débita nostra, salva nos ab igne inferni. Perduc in caelum omnes ánimas, praesertim eas, quae misericórdiae tuae máxime indigent.[17]

HAIL HOLY QUEEN—SALVE REGINA

Hail holy Queen, mother of mercy, our life, our sweetness, and our hope. To thee do we cry, poor banished children of Eve. To thee do we send up our sighs, mourning and weeping in this valley of tears. Turn then, most gracious Advocate, Thine eyes of mercy toward us. And after this our exile show unto us the blessed Fruit of Thy womb, Jesus.

O clement, O loving, O sweet Virgin Mary.

V. Pray for us Holy Mother of God.

R. That we may be made worthy of the promises of Christ.

Salve Regína, mater misericórdiæ; vita, dulcédo, et spes nostra, salve. Ad te Clamámus éxsules fílii Evæ; Ad te Suspirámus, geméntes et flentes in hac lacrimárum valle. Eia ergo, Advocáta nostra, Illos tuos misericórdes óculos ad nos convérte: Et Iesum, benedíctum fructum ventris tui, Nobis post hoc exsílium osténde.

O clemens, o pia, o dulcis Virgo María.

V. Ora pro nobis, Sancta Dei Genetrix.

R. Ut digni efficiamur promissiónibus Christi.

PRAYER AFTER THE ROSARY

Let us pray.

O God, whose only begotten Son, by His life, death, and resurrection, has purchased for us the rewards of eternal life, grant, we beseech Thee, that meditating upon these mysteries of the Most Holy Rosary of the Blessed Virgin Mary, we may imitate what they contain and obtain what they promise, through the same Christ Our Lord. Amen.

Oremus.
Déus, cújus Unigénitus per vítam, mórtem et resurrectiónem súam nóbis salútis ætérnæ præmia comparávit: concéde, quæsumus: ut hæc mystéria sacratíssimo beátæ Maríæ Vírginis Rosário recoléntes, et imitémur quod cóntinent, et quod promíttunt, assequámur. Per eúndem Chrístum Dóminum nóstrum. Amen.

If you benefited from this book, please take a moment to pray a Hail Mary for the author and review this book on amazon.com. I appreciate you and thank you.

Pray the Rosary every day, or you're not on the team.
—Dr. Taylor Marshall

ENDNOTES

[1] Romans 3:24, 6:3.

[2] Taylor R. Marshall, *The Catholic Perspective on Paul: Paul and the Origins of Catholic Christianity.* (Dallas: Saint John Press, 2010).

[3] Blessed Alanus de Rupe, *De Dignitate Psalterii.*

[4] Blessed Alanus de Rupe, *De Dignitate Psalterii.*

[5] Pope Leo XIII, *Octobri Mense,* September 22, 1891.

[6] Pope Leo XIII, *Supremi Apostolatus Officio,* September 1, 1883.

[7] Blessed Alanus de Rupe, *De Dignitate Psalterii.*

[8] The full text of the prayer is: "Open unto us the door of thy loving-kindness, O blessed Mother of God, in that we set our hope on thee, may we not go astray; but through thee may we be delivered from all adversities, fix thou art the salvation of all Christian people."

[9] *Libro en que se tratea de la importancia y exercicio del santo rosario,* Zaragoza: Domingo Portonariis y Ursino (1584), cited after Lorenzo F. Candelaria, *The Rosary Cantoral: Ritual and Social Design in a Chantbook from Early Renaissance Toledo,* University Rochester Press (2008), p. 109.

[10] For Luther's teaching on Mary as Theotokos, see *Martin Luthers Werke, Kritische Gesamtausgabe,* 61 vols., (Weimar: Verlag Hermann Böhlaus Nochfolger, 1883–1983), 21:326, cf. 21:346. For Luther's teaching on the Immaculate Conception, see 52:39.

[11] For details, see *Infiltration: The Plot to Destroy the Church from Within,* by Taylor R. Marshall.

[12] Angelo Stagnaro, "Blessed Bartolo Longo: The Ex-Satanist on the Path to Sainthood," Catholic Herald, 19 July 2011.

[13] For a recommended book on the story and events surrounding Our Lady of Fatima, see William T. Walsh, *Our Lady of Fatima* (New York: Doubleday, 1954).

[14] *Enchiridion of Indulgences,* Sacred Apostolic Penitentiary, Libreria Editrice Vaticana, 1968.

[15] Pope John Paul II, *Rosarium Virginis Mariae,* 19.

[16] Pope John Paul II, *Rosarium Virginis Mariae*, 19.

[17] This is the most commonly used Latin version of the Fatima Prayer. Since the prayer was originally given in Portuguese, there are a variety of versions in circulation.

Made in the USA
Monee, IL
19 January 2021

56623054R00032